C.O.L.O.R.S.

Crossing	A Race
Over	Relations
Lines	Curriculum
Of	
Racial	
Stereotypes	

Designed for regular and alternative high school populations

STUDENT WORKBOOK

Written by
Dr. Michelle R. Jackson

Published by

THE BUREAU ®
FOR AT-RISK YOUTH
PROMOTING GROWTH THROUGH KNOWLEDGE

A Guidance Channel Company
135 Dupont St., P.O. Box 760
Plainview, NY 11803-0760
1-800-99-YOUTH

CONTENTS

C.O.L.O.R.S.

Welcome to C.O.L.O.R.S.

The Philosophy of C.O.L.O.R.S.

We hope you enjoy using this workbook. It is designed not only to be informative, but a little bit of fun too. The C.O.L.O.R.S. curriculum is based on the belief that changing

negative racial attitudes to positive ones is the most important way to improve ethnic relations on our campuses and in our communities. Research and experience show that negative racial attitudes become more positive when people are given the combined opportunity to:

1. honestly and openly discuss racial issues in a safe, constructive environment

2. be formally educated about the causes and dynamics of everyday race-related experiences

3. challenge assumptions and stereotypes about other ethnic groups

4. comfortably interact in a way that helps them recognize common attitudes, beliefs and experiences.

This curriculum works toward creating an environment that will help you recognize similarities, appreciate differences, challenge racial stereotypes, and identify the causes of racial conflict.

The Goals of C.O.L.O.R.S.

We believe that students who seriously approach the activities in this workbook will find themselves experiencing less racial tension at home, at school, and in their community. This is achieved by using lectures, group discussions, and group activities to accomplish the following goals:

Goal #1

Increase your understanding of other ethnic and cultural groups

Goal #2

Stimulate constructive dialogue about controversial and sensitive issues

Goal #3

Question old/false assumptions about other groups

Goal #4

Identify the causes of racism

Goal #5

Identify mechanisms that perpetuate racism

Goal #6

Define key concepts in race relations

Recognizing Concepts

The purpose of this exercise is to learn about the concepts associated with race relations such as "pluralism" and "assimilation" and recognize them when they are portrayed in real life or in literature.

Instructions

Read the passage below.

> Some groups believe that we need to identify which minority behaviors are bad for society and which are good. Then we could explore ways of changing those behaviors so that minorities will be more successful. The assumption appears to be that if minorities could change these behaviors or cultural patterns, racism would be significantly reduced. People in the majority group would be more tolerant of minority behavior, minorities would be more successful, and economic and social justice might prevail. *(Paraphrased from Chesler, 1976)*

Now that you've read the passage, think of what you learned about pluralism and assimilation during class and answer the following question:

Which of the two concepts discussed in class (pluralism and assimilation) is suggested in this passage?

_____

Problems of Integration

This activity will help you explore the difficulties that come along with trying to integrate different groups.

Instructions

Use the space below to list examples of conditions that can make it difficult for different groups to integrate. One column on the worksheet is for writing examples of inappropriate conditions that you have seen or experienced. The other column is for writing possible solutions.

Tellin' It From My Perspective

Examples of Inappropriate Conditions for Integration	Possible Solutions to the Problem

If I Were An Architect

Why are we doing this?

This activity will help you better understand cultural racism.

Instructions:

Using your artistic ability, demonstrate through drawings how the buildings from two different cultures may be structured differently.

Culture: _____

Culture: _____

Now that you have completed your drawings, please answer the following question.

Based on your 2 drawings, is one type of building better than the other? Why?

_____

_____

_____

_____

Experiencing Difference

This activity will help you get in touch with many of the feelings that are associated with being identified as "different."

Instructions

Think of a time in your life when you felt "different" from the people around you. Use the space below to describe that experience. (How old were you? Where were you? Who or what made you feel different?)

I remember when...

_____

_____

_____

_____

_____

_____

_____

_____

_____

_____

_____

_____

_____

How did that experience make you feel? (List 3 adjectives that best describe your feelings.)

1. _____

2. _____

3. _____

Recognizing Theories In Action

Sorry! I can't tell you now, but I promise to tell you after the activity!

Instructions

Here's a bit of trivia that may interest you!

Within the literature on race relations, authors mention that Latinos/Hispanics are excluded from textbooks discussing racism and prejudice. The authors conclude that as a society, we are unfamiliar and unaware of the Latino/Hispanic experience of prejudice and discrimination.

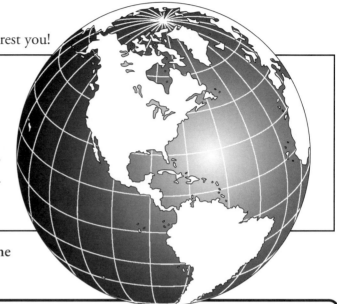

Based on this statement, answer the following questions:

QUESTION #1: Why is there a lack of awareness regarding the Latino experience of prejudice and discrimination?

_____

_____

_____

_____

_____

_____

_____

_____

_____

_____

Your teacher will present Question #2 to the class.

Creating Social Categories

Why are we doing this?

This activity will help you understand how social categories are created.

Instructions

— Name one city on the east coast of the United States: _____

— Name one city on the west coast of the United States: _____

Make a list of the ways that people from the east coast city listed above differ from people in the west coast city listed above.

WEST   EAST

_____   _____
_____   _____
_____   _____
_____   _____
_____   _____
_____   _____
_____   _____
_____   _____
_____   _____
_____   _____
_____   _____

— Name one city in an urban area of the United States: _____

— Name one city in a rural area of the United States: _____

Make a list of the ways that people from the urban city listed above differ from people in the rural city listed above.

URBAN   RURAL

_____   _____
_____   _____
_____   _____

Native American Sayings #1

This activity demonstrates the beauty and insight of many Native American philosophies.

Instructions

Read the saying below and reflect upon it. Use the space provided to explain in your own words what you think the saying is telling us.

"THE HARMONY OF TRUTH"

By Gayle High Pine

The songs and dances and rituals we are given - all our correct movements in the universe - are necessary for it to continue. The Creation is defined by each being as a fish defines the shape of the water, and our every movement sends ripples and waves through it. Nothing exists without its surroundings. We are part of one another, necessary for one another's life. The Creation is One. You have no boundaries. You are the Center. The ripples have no end.

What does this saying mean and what can we learn from it?

_____

_____

_____

_____

_____

Native American Sayings #2

This activity demonstrates the beauty and insight of many Native American philosophies.

Instructions

Read the saying below and reflect upon it. Use the space provided to explain in your own words what you think the saying is telling us.

"THE ROAD BACK TO OUR FUTURE"

By Sakokwenonkwas *(A sub-chief of the Bear Clan of the Mohawk Nation)*

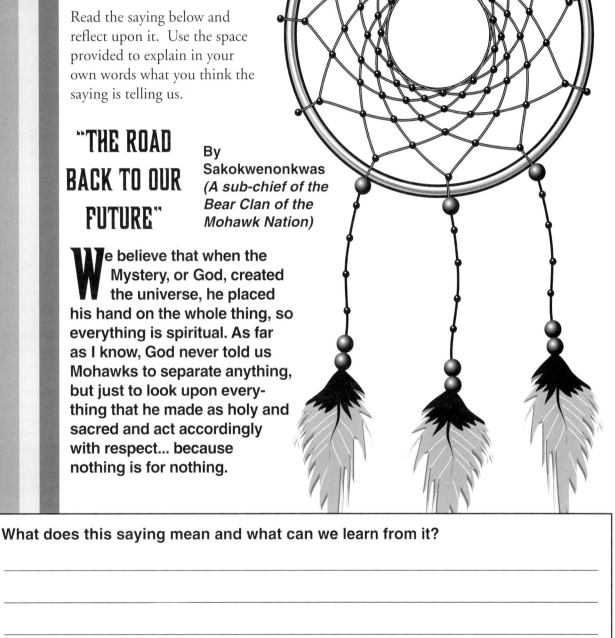

We believe that when the Mystery, or God, created the universe, he placed his hand on the whole thing, so everything is spiritual. As far as I know, God never told us Mohawks to separate anything, but just to look upon everything that he made as holy and sacred and act accordingly with respect... because nothing is for nothing.

What does this saying mean and what can we learn from it?

_____

_____

_____

_____

_____

Native American Sayings #3

This activity demonstrates the beauty and insight of many Native American philosophies.

Read the saying below and reflect upon it. Use the space provided to explain in your own words what you think the saying is telling us.

"THE ROAD BACK TO OUR FUTURE"

By Sakokwenonkwas

(A sub-chief of the Bear Clan of the Mohawk Nation)

We are trying to bring people together in a spiritual union, but not together in a big physical union... He *(God)* told you this was our Mother Earth - He didn't just tell it to the Indian. He told it to everybody and that's going to be our common denominator to peace.

What does this saying mean and what can we learn from it?

_____

_____

_____

_____

_____

Acting Out The Stereotypes

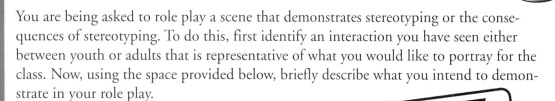

Why are we doing this?

This activity will help you understand the power of stereotyping.

Instructions

You are being asked to role play a scene that demonstrates stereotyping or the consequences of stereotyping. To do this, first identify an interaction you have seen either between youth or adults that is representative of what you would like to portray for the class. Now, using the space provided below, briefly describe what you intend to demonstrate in your role play.

Scene **1** | Take **1** | Director

Description

Now that you have decided what you would like to role play, here are some questions about stereotyping that you may want to consider. Wait for your instructor to tell you when to write down your responses. Use a separate sheet of paper for your answers.

Question #1: Which of the principals of stereotyping that were taught in your lesson are portrayed in your role play?

Question #2: How do the concepts and experiences seen in your role play apply to gang involvement?

Question #3: How do the concepts and experiences seen in your role play apply to conflicts that occur on your school campus or in your community?

Examining Cross-Cultural Communications

Why are we doing this?

This activity will help you better recognize the verbal and nonverbal behaviors we use to communicate with individuals who speak a different language.

Instructions

Use the space provided to answer the questions listed below.

What kinds of <u>verbal</u> behavior do you use to communicate with someone who speaks a different language? (Example: talking loud)

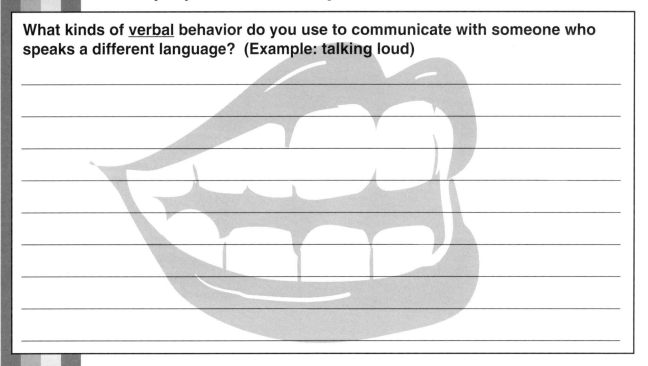

What kinds of <u>nonverbal</u> behavior do you use to communicate with someone who speaks a different language? (Example: Using hand gestures)

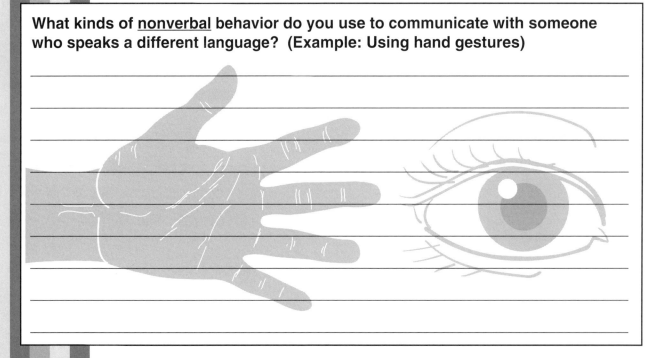

Exploring Your Origins

Why are we doing this?

This activity will help you gain a greater understanding and appreciation for your history and heritage.

Instructions

Identify something you and/or your family does that is characteristic of your culture and find out where/how that characteristic originated. (You are expected to read outside literature in your search for the answer).

Describe the cultural characteristic you are researching.

_____

_____

_____

_____

Use the space below to describe how and where your cultural characteristic originated. (List at least one source where your information was found.)

_____

_____

_____

_____

_____

_____

_____

_____

_____

_____

_____

_____

GLOSSARY

Assimilation - To absorb into the culture of a population or group.

Case Study - A carefully drawn biography that may be gathered through interviews, questionnaires, and/or psychological tests.

Culture - A framework for behavior that provides order to how groups of people relate to one another and to their world.

Cultural Pluralism - The state of society in which members of diverse ethnic, racial, religious, or social groups independently develop and participate in their traditional cultures within the confines of a common civilization.

Cultural Racism - One cultural group's belief that their accomplishments and creativity are superior to those of other groups because of racial differences.

Diversity - The condition of being different or having differences.

Discrimination - The act or practice of making a difference in treatment or favor based on something other than individual merit.

Ethnic Group - Of or relating to races or large groups of people classed according to common traits and customs.

Exclusion - The state of being excluded.

Inclusion - The state of being included.

Individual Racism - Individual thoughts, feelings, and behaviors that develop from a belief that one type of person is genetically superior, and a different type of person is genetically inferior.

In-Group - The group you belong to.*

Institutional Racism - Practices followed by institutions, either intentionally or unintentionally, which perpetuate inequality based on preconceived ideas about racial groups.

Integration - The act or process of incorporating equals into a society, an organization, or other groups or institutions.

Mainstream Culture - The culture identified as having the most significant influence on the values, standards, and activities of a society.

Minority - A part of a population that differs from other parts in some way and is often treated differently.

Out-Group - Individuals in a different group.*

Paralanguage - The tone, pitch, stress, volume, and speed with which language is spoken.

Pluralism - A state of society in which members of different ethnic, racial, religious, or social groups participate in and develop their own unique culture or special interests within the confines of a common civilization.

Prejudice - An irrational attitude of hostility directed against an individual, a group, a race, or their supposed characteristics.

Racism - A belief that race is the primary factor that determines human traits and capacities and that racial differences produce the inborn superiority of a particular race.

Stereotypes - A fixed notion or concept of a group, person, idea, etc. held by a number of people which allows for no individuality.

Definitions refer to the context in which the term is used in C.O.L.O.R.S. curriculum and are not universal definitions.